Natur
and
Design

Written by Pippa Goodhart

Collins

Animals, birds and trees were here long before people and we can learn a lot from them.

gecko

500,000,000 years ago

200,000,000

shark

termite

Let's see what nature has taught
us about how to design things.

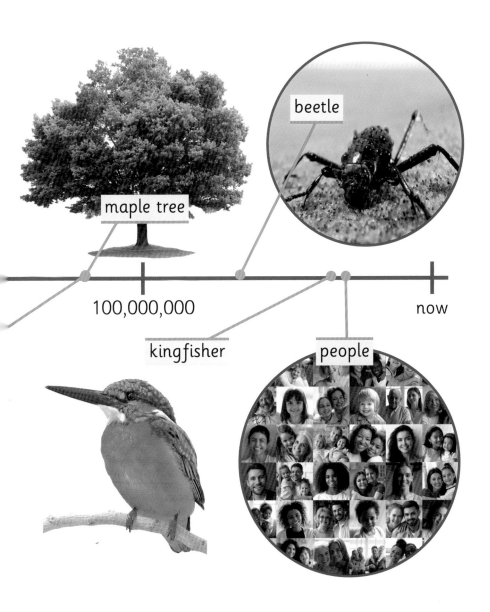

beetle

maple tree

100,000,000

now

kingfisher

people

Great white sharks are silent, quick swimmers.
This makes them great hunters. Their special skin
makes them extra fast.

great white shark

Shark skin has tiny v-shaped scales called dermal denticles. The denticles make water flow over skin more smoothly so sharks can cut through the water with ease.

dermal denticles

Engineers have copied dermal denticles to make a range of things work more efficiently.

A swimmer wearing an outfit with dermal denticles swims faster.

This coating for aircraft helps them move through the air more easily.

If maple seeds fell straight under the tree, they wouldn't have room to grow. So maple seeds have blades to catch the wind, spinning them far away from the tree.

The shape of these maple seeds has taught engineers the best design for turbine blades.

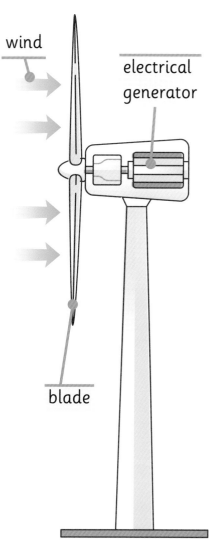

wind

electrical generator

blade

Humpback whales can weigh as much as four double-decker buses, and yet are agile swimmers. Their flippers have bumps along one edge that make them more efficient.

10

Water and air flow more efficiently between bumps than over a straight edge. So, turbine blades were made with bumps to help them take more energy from the wind.

turbine blade

The air gets hotter in daytime and colder at night, but soil changes temperature more slowly.
Soil is good **insulation**, so some animals make their homes underground.

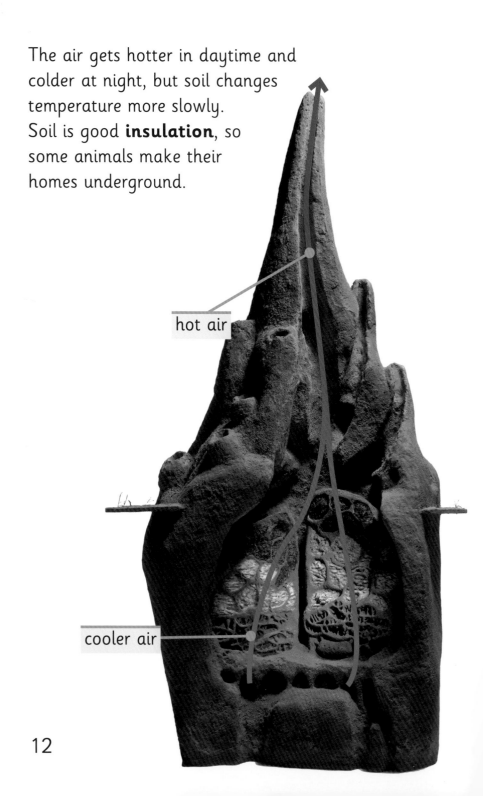

hot air

cooler air

Termites live in nests constructed underground, with a tall tower above. Hot air rises, pulling cooler air in below. That air **circulation** gives the nest **ventilation** and regulates the temperature.

This tower copies termite-nest cooling and heating. Fans help air circulation, pulling fresh air in from below. Stale air escapes through chimneys at the top.

hot air

cooler air

Some beetles have a good solution to a very
dry environment. They stick their bottoms up,
and fog is caught on tiny bumps on their waxy skin.
The fog droplets pour down into the beetle's mouth.

bumpy skin

In these dry mountains, people hang nets to catch damp foggy air. Water droplets pour down into tanks.

damp air

bumpy surface

Bullet trains made a roaring sonic boom noise coming out of tunnels. Scientists looked to nature for a solution.

Engineers studying kingfishers saw how their pointed heads and beaks go into water with hardly a splash. So they designed the trains to be more pointed and streamlined.

Geckos can climb up sheer walls without falling off.
Their toes have hundreds of microscopic bristles that
can stick and unstick.

These special boots and gloves copy the microscopic bristles on gecko toes. They enable people to climb walls.

Nature has been a great inspiration for us, helping us to create amazing things.

Glossary

circulation flow of air or liquid

insulation a layer that stops something getting
  hotter or colder

ventilation keeping air flowing

Future designs?

Humpback whales surround shoals of fish with bubbles that act like a net. Then they eat the fish.

Could we learn to fish with bubble nets instead of plastic ones, to help the environment?

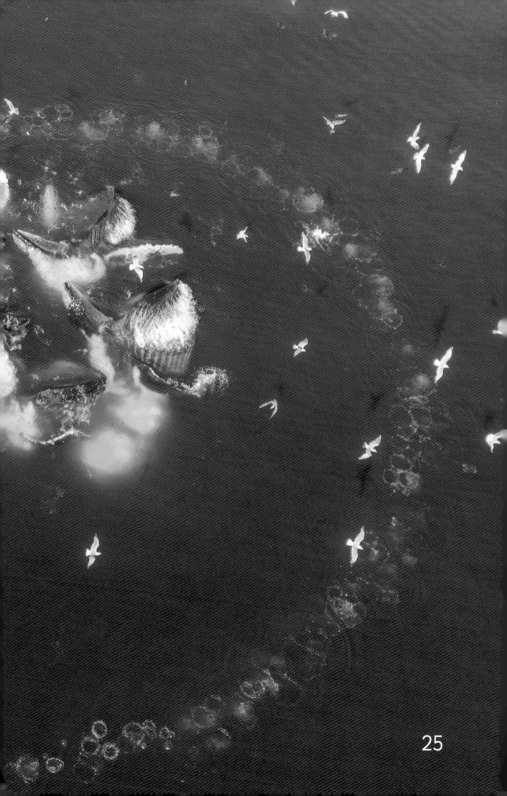

25

Fly like a squirrel!

Unusual flaps of skin between legs and arms let flying squirrels glide between trees.

Wing suits copy that shape, letting people jump from planes to glide almost 20 miles.

Geckos inspire space design

Engineers are creating robots with a stickiness inspired by gecko feet to repair satellites and collect space junk.

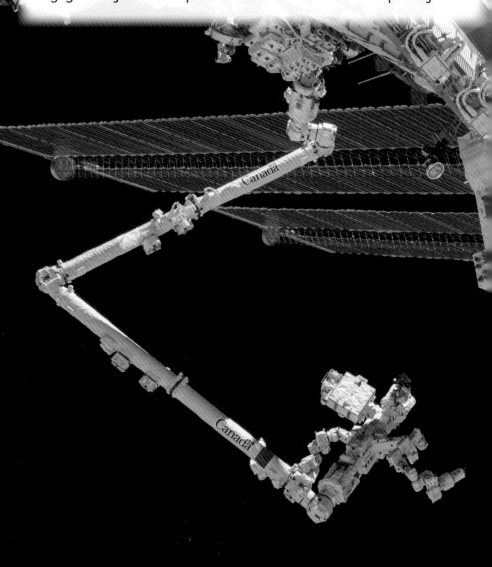

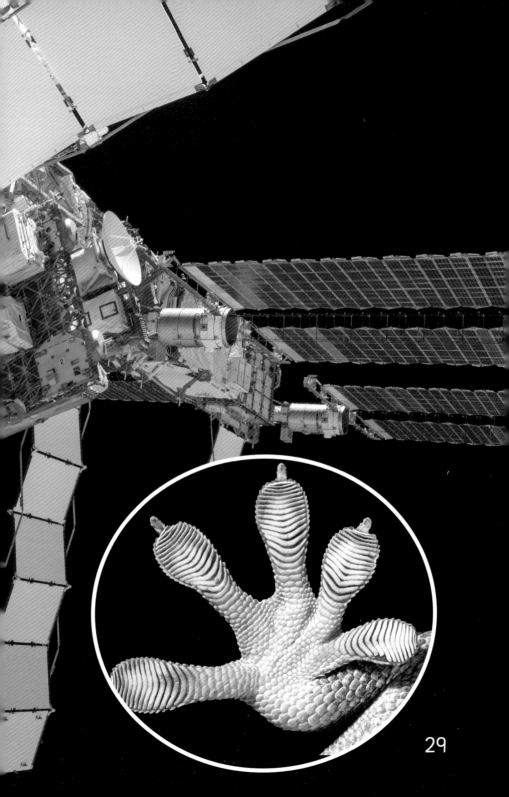

Nature inspiring design

Review: After reading

Use your assessment from hearing the children read to choose any GPCs, words or tricky words that need additional practice.

Read 1: Decoding

- Ask the children to read these words. Tell them to find the pairs of words that share the same long vowel sound.
  great   caught   engineers   weigh   here   more
- Challenge the children to read these words aloud as smoothly and fluently as they can. Say: Can you blend in your head when you read these words?
  circulation   insulation   ventilation

Read 2: Prosody

- Model pausing for commas as you read page 12.
- Say: I wonder how it would sound without the commas. Model reading page 12 without pausing and discuss how the meaning is less clear.
- Encourage the children to read page 13, experimenting by reading the page incorrectly (not pausing at commas) and then correctly (pausing at commas) to hear how pausing helps the listener understand.

Read 3: Comprehension

- Reread page 20 and ask: Have you learnt elsewhere about other animals with cleverly designed body features? What are they able to do? (e.g. *spiders' feet that don't get stuck on webs; camouflage colours to hide*)
- Turn to pages 18 and 19 and discuss the connection between the kingfisher and the bullet train. Ask the children for other ideas in the book that back up this statement: "Engineers learn a lot from nature."
- Challenge the children to skim the book for the right pages, read them and offer a summary of the link between nature and an engineer's design. Say: What is the link between:
  o sharks and swimsuits? (*pages 4 to 6 – both use dermal denticles to help with fast swimming*)
  o whale flippers and turbine blades? (*pages 10 and 11 – both have a bumpy edge for efficiency*)
- Ask the children to use pages 30 and 31 to prepare a few sentences on the connections between nature and people's designs. Volunteers could read their sentences to the class.
- Bonus content: Look together at pages 24 to 27. Which of the ideas on these pages do the children think is most interesting? Why?